The Stations Of The Day

Michael W. Thomas

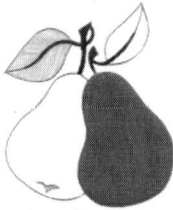

Black Pear Press

The Stations Of The Day

First published 2019 by **Black Pear Press Limited**
www.blackpear.net

A CIP catalogue record of this book is available from the British Library

Where people may be identifiable, every effort has been made to share the relevant poem with them before publication.

ISBN 978-1-910322-97-0

Cover photographs: Lynda Prescott and Michael W. Thomas

To Lynda
As Always

Contents

1: A Rose...

Only A Rose

Only a rose
in an area window
telling the tale
of a sportive yesterday

or pressed in haste on someone
by somebody else in a bar
who'd been stood up but even so
wished love to dance over the evening

the rose knows nothing
of what it was meant to say
how it was dressed to say it
all it wants

is to sing back the glow of the moon
which never says what it's said to say either
but happily listens while nosing apart
the dark of the rose's room

fixing the way an old-gold blouse
pours down the back of a chair
the way a clock-hand
tickles the low hours

only a rose
only a moon
doing what nobody sees

free from mortal chat
of urge and contrition
in all the old co-opted places
platform calendar bluff

if the rose dreams
it's of rain's delirium
arching clear
of its birth-soil

if the moon dreams
it's of birthing its own light
no more the cold courier
of sun-sweat

2: When You Were Young…

Almost

(1960)

When you were young, a thousand helpless miles
lay between, say, the tenth of December
and Christmas—which stood there, mule-indifferent,
knowing fine it had you fast in its heart,

that even now you heard the morning roads,
the last shunt in the fire-pluming night
as other than the regulated drone
your breath and bones were made of. Round the school,

on stony faces of alcoved torment
in Friday church, the iron air thinned out
and lifted: something else drew on, ahead
of fidget-arsed nativities, tea-towels

on kingly crewcuts, cards of solder-glue.
Time softened, the blood rose to its face. Bells
almost rang beneath the hoosh of buses,
the clouds were undersides of magic ways

where angels got into first position,
shepherds took form in sputnik-space, prepared
to be unprepared, mithering, scared stiff.
Then all at once the last Wednesday of term

with the ex-Navy barber (Dads and Lads),
and you high in the chair, buffed, clippered, set
to meet the only land you loved. Mirrored,
the brushings of the dead year fell like snow.

Amber

(1961)

In our house
there was only one light,
living amber and dry
in the wireless.

Melody on the Move
pushed us out into the world
each comical English morning—
a wittery tumble

of pizzicato strings,
jolly-dee imperial.
Mom and Dad
went off to do a little more

among the noise and fiddle
of their trades,
then came home and took out
the day's theft of their hearts

on each other and on me.
The primary school I went off to
was a left-behind
stuck between smoke and depot.

Miss Stott, the Headmistress,
was peppered with brooches
like a high, wide barrel
furbelowed in tar.

Mrs Dale wore blister-lens glasses
that made her words even stupider.
I shall smack, warned Miss Stott,
and Mrs Dale did, like breathing.

I got the trick
of staring in a not-staring way
till the pair of them
burst into flames.

David Fitzgerald last had a wash
in his mom's amniotic sauna.
Delia Inskip was a mom from the off,
one of the few souls I've known

who was kind in the way
the sky blues down at sunset:
a gift like a peeking face
amid the clouts on the ear,

the Friday fish,
the fidget-pit of church:
Lamb of God
Who takes away the sins of the world

I'm done in
and can't get Mrs Dale
past a Regulo two smoulder.
Help me out.

Patrick McHale was sweat-crust cheery,
Bernard Page was malevolent and thick,
Catherine Weir burlesqued
with the pin of her tartan skirt.

But John Muldoon, now,
he could ape Harold MacMillan,
so I fed him patter-lines
till Mrs Dale was on us,

her glasses that close
like gormless moons
double-whammying
a peaceful earth at graze.

5

In the evenings,
when dad was on the piss
and mom's television soiled the air
with bow-tied execution fodder,

I'd sit in the kitchen by the wireless,
pilot the amber dial with the sound off.
Hilversum, Geneva, Bonn. Realms.
Never-nevers. Intimations—

like country-scene woodcuts
you'd see in the *Radio Times*.
Dells. Sculpted ploughland.
Otherwheres.

I'd ape John Muldoon
like the snake-belt bard he was,
narrate myself back to being born again
and growing up in such proper places,

laughing for the peal of it,
crying just to thank,
standing on a ridgeway
with non-stare stare at speed

till this house and the England around it
ballooned and exploded and ashed away.

Reg At Hawksyard

(Spring camp, 1967)

Reg Reynolds had need
to murder us over and over.
We were cod-gentry. This one's dad
had staggered use of a lease-lend Zodiac.
That mom's name trailed letters
whiffy with fortitude and Savlon.

We went home to trainer-lawns
house-names chamfered to distress
a better class of bootmark
from the kids across the way. Reg
got sucked down a long low lane
vanished into the last pot on the left
where the road
fell into excavated footings.

Bull's eyes and a face out of temper
he was keeper of his tribe's disgruntlements:
an uncle barged off a Hobart liner
handed back his pom's ten pounds in singles
with a brace of Windsor smirks. Dad
throwing shapes nightly
savagely
along between the Fox Inn and Matterhorn Mavis.

A May morning. Camp struck at Hawksyard
the past five days furled
under green zips and Ministry stencil.
Skip tamping the bell-cropped grass
with the look of a cornered bear
Bosun suppling his knots
the kind that rigged the world fast
against Johnny future

us lot
like knackered magi
driving crate and roll before us

7

to where Reg
high on the tailgate
hooshed them into the lorry's dark
as you'd heave coal against the flank of winter.

Our thirst leadened the canvas
we lost our grip and cried monkey-shrill
on the air. Blame got under our vests
pebbled our instep. Reg
netted all the sky in his grin
swigged his bottle of pop which
recorked
was snugged behind his boot

he heard our thirst
and saw behind its pleas our teatime tables
the lives that we drank from petrol-offer glasses
that we breathed with a hint of Alpine whatever
saw us far from Hawksyard
scrubbed up to reach the dimple of godliness
uncaring that he'd be out of sight
at the clank-end of the chain.

Wordless he hooshed
and finished his pop. For one sun-medallioned hour
he owned us. He tilted history that-a-way
made its pen write of things newly
as gentlemen may write between gasps
of a race with heads under their shoulders

soon to be scribbled out of course—
back where right was wrong
like the sums he could never untie
the regal names he kept on fluffing
where we'd wait in our ranks
until he'd been summoned again
hauled out of the door
to breast the latest home calamity
and only then would say *Good morning, Miss.*

Ed Poultney Put Me Straight

(January 1969)

You suck up to him, then you slag him off
behind his back. Not a philosopher, Ed,
not even a lover of handkerchiefs,
but he told it as it had long been
with me and Nikko Benson. A funny way
Ed's words had. Once they were out,
they sort of doubled back, so you felt you'd heard them
and not. Maybe that was just this fifteen year-old's mind,
onto the next thing, the next and next. Who on earth
could live and hear in the moment when the best
was up ahead and all to be strained for? But later they'd return,
his words, at your neck like rain on the walk home
from school. So it was with his take
on how I treated Nikko… and others, too,
though I guessed Ed knew that I knew that he didn't need
to say.

      Friday, January 17th, the last day of our mid-year exams.
I'd had one first thing, before break, with the last
due up after lunchtime. So between half-eleven and lunch
I was sitting by the window, studying a book of poems,
which is to say, testing the give of my chair and staring out
at hillocky grassland and feeder roads looping round
the end of the Sixties. They crept back then, nudging aside
the half-a-leagues and foreign fields on the page:
You suck up to him, then you slag him off
behind his back. I'd got nowhere to run, no music
to jump into, nothing to anything at all. They found me
and as they did I stopped. *Finish the sentence you're writing,*
I'd heard all week and would hear again,
last time, that afternoon. Without a thought,
I finished the way I was being. Though still sat
coaxing whimpers from the legs of my chair,
I climbed out of me and through the window,
got down onto the winter grassland
and looked back up at me leaning to that book.

For the very first time I saw myself
as another figure on a ground, like all the rest
in that room and the other rooms and the other roads,
the houses, the towns, the everywheres. My suck-up,
slag-off words made a difference, whispered Ed—
they nipped, pinched, came all over gassy
like a beaker tipped up in a lab. They baffled
and they pained and, though I may down the line
say the same or worse, they weren't proper.

      I climbed back into myself,
turned a page to find the earnest font
extolling a skylark. I was never the same after.
At lunchtime I sought Ed Poultney out,
ham-fisted my way to thanks. He lifted his duffel-bag
off its peg and snugged it to his shoulder.
And frowned. *You what?* Frowned again.
Ah, well…that carry-on just don't suit you…
up to you, though…eh? Take or leave.

Bikes

(July 1969. For Mike Evans, 1953-2014)

We stood smack in the middle of summer,
felt the minutes, hours, days flow down our skin.
A crazy bunch of miles above, some man
was set to trampoline about the moon
and get himself misheard by history.
The sun was our manor. We swung our bikes
along its beams, its paths and cut-throughs, out
across the molten ways of housing schemes,
where peace begged for a chance from open doors
and windows sang of pinball wizardry.
No freedom for the man up on the moon,
no change of gear or bush-grassed gulley. He
was parked before the world, a black-white moth
netted with one wing twitching. We roared on.
He jumped stiff-legged, a toddler testing beds.
We slicked our tyres with ancient oil. He coped
as best he could with ice-white silence, left
a flag to be unloved by July breeze.

Did we feel autumn in our bones as we
rode home, hear time complaining at the snow?
Course not: we'd been bowling over fire,
chasing sunspots like rooks. Our transmissions
were simple as a breath, joy to muscle
to speed to joy to muscle—the right stuff.
Meanwhile, beyond the day, the moon man tried
to get back up a ladder as unsound
as those our dads ascended, bulb in hand,
mithering of expense and foreign tat,
while far below our mothers gripped the rungs
and tuned their minds' dial elsewhere, to their times
of joy, of speed and fire, endless sun.

Twopenn'orth

(September 1969)

After his first few short years
he reached inside his heart
and gave the world back its twopenn'orth.
Left for school in new shoes
and good time on the first day
of the autumn term, briefcase filled
with a book or two and several changes
of life. Slowed at the gates while his pals
flowed on, while teachers in puttering gear
squeezed and chided through.

All that tagged salmon
rising for the weir.

He walked backwards,
got in under the fir trees
at the end of a run of new-build detacheds,
each with its car, a couple with an extra bit
thin-scree'd in Spanish tile.
This is what making it means,
he'd been told, though years later
he'd know what he dumbly felt
right then, that making it
is inching up a winter twig
as best you can with crossed fingers.

He was told, too, at the end of July
that he'd have to work like stink.
Now he strips off the only stinks
he's ever known, stares a moment
at the creases of the boy by other minds
confected, folds it all up
and stows it for the hedgehogs
to shred into nests.

Naked, he leans to the hesitant weather,
feels on his skin the prickle-change
as veto, bribe and homily shut down.
Opens the briefcase, drops the books
for the hedgehogs' wonder
and slowly re-togs in the colours of
hereon in, the blind bends he can nearly see,
the slamming door he nearly hears
that springs another open.

School begins. Figures run the length
of a bell's insistence. Through the fir trees
he fancies that all of it un-mushrooms
and dies in tangerine smoke. Hears
his own smile as one long parched of love.
Knows the plenitude of winds out there,
how one carries you like angels
and another dips for your shins.
The hedgehogs can have the case
for surprise overnighters. Straightening,
he turns, wobbles into his first clean walk,
beyond the Spanish refuges, beyond
the instruction and rebuke
of a thousand slow murders.

Motor Shakes

Time was, I had the motor shakes. At night
I'd take the streets and precincts with my arms
at spasm, the muscles of my neck out
in blades. I made the very rain think twice
before it fell. You'd think I needed to
disorder nature, was hotfoot for fields
of strawed and settled horses to break up
in foaming, shock-maned circles, terrified.

I had a heart of old, cold ashes then:
my mother and my father. All about
my skin and nerves the lights would go on as
she carped in my gizzard, he chuted down
my veins. I had to get God's own move on
to keep them shoved apart, so their old songs
of battle would shrill back to where they'd do
no harm, in some small corner of my breath.

But sometimes they would meet face to face in
my heart and stage again their endless nights
of slam and clatter. She would pull aside
a blood-black thicket, remonstrate, demand
housekeeping or a little pick of love—
while he execrated the day the winds
deserted him between voluptuous port
and sun-prinked embraceable horizon.

They're long gone now. My way from avenue
to bypass to lane is paced and chosen
as I wish. My heart busies itself with
its neaps and springs in quiet. I may surprise
the dog-fox or the hare along the track
but I stand scarecrow-loose and hold their eyes
with mine and whisper, pass, friend, or be still
as I am. Share this tick of time. They're gone.

Two In A Seizure

(October 1999)

And I saw my dad
after twenty years gone wide

as two strangers might stand their evening down
find themselves watering adjacent bushes

an autumn coincidence:
him in the town's remaining pub
me after a quick glass of water
halfway down a long, long road

there he sat
hair crimped from insistent smoke
splits crying in the boards beneath his chair

stirring in his head maybe
a de Kuyper and Capstan Full Strength past
stout re-enactments

meat-and-two-veg sleeps
while Sundays clouded and the curtains breathed his sweat

elbows and mouth and night barneys
tosses argued in their season

till one fat wet word too many
changed the locks
with mom tight against them
firing back at last
doll-tiny and suddenly huge

there he sat, his ages blue upon his flesh
weeping time as from a split sack

we saw each other with hares' eyes
two in a shared seizure

15

I waited for him
to flutter down through the boards
perhaps he did the same

either way our hands would never find
the brow-stroke salute that he
old salt
had schooled me in
when I was young and bowling off
and he'd ask where I was bound for

I left my water
he might be there still

half-risen and wondering why—
unexercised by piss after all

the pint before him
glinting off his dreams:

easy-peasy Matterhorns
skewered windmills
suns for the eclipsing
after a Sunday kip

3: Where Nothing's Asked Or Thieved...

Victoria Street

(Wolfville, Nova Scotia, December)

The shortest day, in a season and place
where shortness can't be measured anyway.
All afternoon the snow has waved downhill,
bulging the corners of the five or six
flung houses between up here on the heights
and Main Street far below, a river lost.
How stopped it is, how soft at ten to five,
with everyone back home or trying hard—
the slew and rev of cars unheard from here
like graceless souls along the Kentville Road
or howling through New Minas. One's got through
off to the right way down the flurried slope,
unless it never left. A sudden wind
heaps white in scarps and foothills on its hood,
dresses its red charge-cable in mint pearl.
Give it an hour, a half, the car will be
an ice-bomb with an endless cartoon fuse.

The snow lays off the senses and the blood.
Behind, above the heights, a march of pines
must be conferring as they've always done
in creak and brush—but no word reaches here.
Each flake finds boot, cloth, waterproof, as if
pretending to be moments of an age—
so melts, so lingers. Day is just a tale,
the pines are shadows that once thought in green,
the houses down the slope were never there.
Gone five now, surely, even six, and still
the heavens tighten and unmake. Someone
somehow gets out and calls and calls. But still
each moment falls and is and ends and falls.

Elliot Street

(Saskatoon, Saskatchewan, December)

A small clearing some hundred yards or so
from city traffic. In another place,
a village green. Triangular, guarded
by year-end snow, the fingerbones of trees.

My place, my country. I come here each day
to watch the snow uneven out, the chase
of fog mites in the clearing-lamp, to hear
the ghost leaves of old Augusts at their talk.

Beyond, the morning and the evening cars
hoot and fishtail through the trees, but mostly
all's quiet as fidelity and lets
the stations of the day move softly by.

I've tried where the cars go. A traveller could
do worse than happen on a space like this
where nothing's asked or thieved, where the bitters
of time unsour and fall beneath the snow.

In Ballyroe

(Kilfinane, Co. Limerick)

In Ballyroe I look at a roadside fence
below a lawned rise and rounded ship's-bridge windows.
Up the way other houses are snug to the verge
or ride the outwaves of the Ballyhoura hills—
down, a stream thins on between brows of marshgrass
which bind or loosen the south Limerick damp.
The town then, announced by a Church of Ireland wall
much-fettled, a finger post that says 'House of Music'
and points to a martyr's iron tears.

Before I was born I came from here
but I lived in places of soot,
of cold that unmakes the pulse,
in brown forever Sunday places
with curtains bunched in window gaps
and gates without sure catches. I entertained
moon- and frying-pan faces, unlaughed lips,
huckstering eyes, voices that promised the length of the road
then ghosted away at a bend.

All the while, I guess, the church wall
breathed birdsong, the finger post urged music
on black windows, dogs with appointments
at town-end bins, the An Post van tight-circling
from Noonan's pumps and coal.

I look again far up, far down. A starling initiates
the mobbing of a roof. Light flashes through my years,
dim or blinding, as in a drunken storm,
as in a message fizzed from wire to wire
that hides the odd pick of sense
in lengths and widths of a language
that has never found its country or its breath.

Middlefield Lane

(Hagley, Worcestershire)

You'd stroll along it. To dash for a train
or vanishing appointment would mean boots
hard down on precinct slabs of coarse yellow—
not this fall-away turn from the main road
in all its nipping fury. Here's a world
that keeps itself forgotten beyond lawns
of tidiness played off against the briar,
beneath tiled overhangs, on porches where
eyes glance between paused hands and cryptic clues.
Couples still walk out here. He bulks his tie,
she says again the beetle-drive will go
just swimmingly, her parents want him there,
why would they not? Gosh, he's an ass. Apples
hang full and scrumpable into the road,
teasing the reach of the nurse's youngest
who even now is mooching to the bad.
Look, that stone cherub's been rain-worked enough
but smiles on brokenly with half a bow.
Now comes the curate, rugger-red, tending
on foot (that bike, eh? someone conned him blind).

Stay here. Back in the roar there are no words
and so no stories. Any dazzle is
a spasm of a hand on match on stone.
You could walk to the lane's last swans-neck lamp,
still casting light from lived and drifted years,
and lean upon a field-gate. At your back,
the supple runs of chat, *good evenings* looped
round latches, cracks about the padre's bike.
Ahead, an old-gold stack, a path that feints
and ponders between wood and rise. Perhaps
there will be new stories, waiting on words
to sound in leaf and stone. If not, here's place
and moment anyway, the same low breeze
that parted time before footings, garden,
beetle-drive, craved apple, porch. It's enough.

20

Shrawley Cross

(Worcestershire, Christmas Day)

They left just before you got there. That's how
the air feels, calming down after the last
scritch of a cart-wheel, protest of a van
suitcased and mattress-laden. Some on foot,
switching a cow's rump, kicking chubby-kneed
through rut water, or marching on alone
with careful, unmarried bearing, bedroll
beneath one arm, a patching-bag—the sum
of what they'll offer to first light elsewhere.
The drudge and muscle of the years cleared out:
smock, forge-apron, sponsored high-vis whatnot.

Silence moves in on the crossroads, around
the bus-shelter, a chimney vague in trees.
It's as though nature straightens for a while,
done with the need to pick up and shift over.
For the first time you hear how nothing breathes,
the song of nowhere birds from end to end
as the world carries on not passing through
and a day-moon only means itself, no more.

Young Lovers In Roseville

(The Black Country, 1975)

This remains
the drab-glam three-day life

the Fifties at least were honest
turned out shallow pockets

confessed without pressing
that yesterday ran off with the paints

she still finds confetti
when she sits at her mom's replaced dresser
curves a mirror round her nape
like a radiation gun

little land
spavined by fatman history

but pledged to cripple on in dad's boots
hooked and eyed in a New England

his ribs are still raw
from velveteen elbows
between the lych-path
and the flock of old tin cans

Roseville is nice
carriage lamps
come early to porch-frames
before they're suppled and dried

but the people sigh their colours
from their faces and their clothes

Instamatics catch this truly
but decades on are called cheap

22

he hears the chat
on the Wolverhampton bus
a job's come up in Bloxwich

suddenly he's travelling
with adversarial mullets

Julian is a good name
says her mother
or otherwise Christobel
as though something posh
can rout the future

Wolverhampton was
the workshop of the world
it said so on the franking
to the left of her head

just the fitments now
a bit of a counter out front
remnants at cost

the Bloxwich job
goes to a mate
who changes pubs.

Waiting at the decade's end
something that really does mean it
heels back a little more each time
against its brittle chain.

Ashchurch For Tewkesbury

(September equinox, 1989)

Just as we pull in
the evening breaks across the hills.
Shadows quit their stalls
and blood the land.

The sun re-angles
the last of its work. Houses on the slopes
are barns burning, platform fences
are spears racked for a volley.

Even the carriage's *door open* beep
is a call to cleansing, even the hikers
who climb aboard pack flame
about their eyes, their bottle-hooks.

A mile or so ahead are nightfall embankments,
a tunnel the colour of cold. But the sun
makes like noon, swells into us
through seat and window. We don't move.

Landing

(Stourport-on-Severn, 2015)

The bookshelves face the stairs. A shadow falls
across the spines, the usual mix of scuffed,
prize, unread. Top row right, one's been half-wedged
and angled up: somebody's passing glance
or, full of sprightly words, riffled through for
a speech, a turn. Nearby, a night-light, round
as a carved eye, which may glow orange like
a household star, or blue, a bud snipped from
ocean meadows. Further away, something
clicks and thrums. The sound fills the landing with
electric snow, settling deep on the rug,
streaking an island framed in serious wood.
The walls fidget as snow gives way to heat
while round the corner the bathroom cord swings
a bit. A window open? All is calm.
A fat towel coiling off a door-side rail?
No flump. Anyway, that's another world
or none at all. The only thing it gives
to here is a striped lighthouse—the cord-pull
in and out of sight beside the books, which
slows, shows two stripes, one stripe, a flash until
it isn't, save as a commotion caught
in no head, stilled by no hand. The thrum stops.
Time gazes on the island, the wedged book.

Saturday Evening Houses In Summer

Saturday evening houses in summer
are all the go with pans and crockery
fed to the sink a flash of bus window
predicting out-of-season players massed
for the next stop brimful with pride with pain
but either way half-cut the table smells
of Indian or fish thin out beneath
the upstairs perfumes talcs the dresser-mess
wardrobes blown wide controlled explosions
of tops and knickers soon a thousand towns
will be turned over to the taxi-freight
of token ties alpine hems splendid lungs
till hours on a million mobile screens
skim through the dark like moonflakes

                                  meanwhile those
becalmed in Saturday evening houses
confect distraction through other screens with
twenty year old rural bloodbaths or some
natty-pastel guide hopping trains from Rhyl
to Bangalore soon enough the taxis
will slow for drives and junctions abandon
the skewed the disassembled

                         already
the houses are growing their Sunday skin
to suffer the drag of car-boot lugging
feel retail routes unfurled the quickened breath
of churchyard grasses on the up and up

Glebe

I wonder what it's like
to live by a glebe. You'd lead
a woodcut life, I suppose.
People passing in the lane
would say hulloa on their way
to see their children play catch
as catch can. Am not
would be amn't. I'd need to know
the ins and outs of Bristol fashion
not Bristol passion as I'd thought
which must be to do with slavers docking
and merchants' daughters running
for their lives. I'd have to be prepared
for old parties in ruinous hats
who'd say see-now
tell all the year's weather
from a blemish on a pine (though
at home where no-one could see
they might dress as corn-factors
and read Goethe). I'm guessing
I'd have to lean on a stile
despite there being
a county-wide geometry of fences
that could as easily bear the weight
of my twilit brown study.

To myself though
I would still think of asbestosis
murders in city basements
how people are told to aspire
which is posh for stay put
how their honest money is fucked
like a daughter on a shore
caught gazing too long
out over the Bristol roads
who is now torn
who is now bone-broken.

Unmapped

Here is a country road
blocked with rubble a few yards in

so it does not know
its journey any more
cannot call back sky and incident
from all the years

the buttoned feet
that tapped along it
Sundays in their close white chafe
petrol blush upon the leaves
when someone got out and got under
a Vespa lamp stinging the dusk

it cannot look up now
from its bends
at how tree-tops net the seasons
in stars of summer blood
and Christmas pearl

a bird sits on the rubble
looks inland
at the onwardness as was

the stroke on a map
each day more not there
sunk a touch deeper
through the tides of the earth

Travellers

They are made of mist, a seasoned need
to step light and thin round
the mires of the world. The ends
of unlettered roads will find them,
possibly, if a caravan rocks its green roof,
betrays that it is not after all
the high skirt of midsummer.

But the first steeps of autumn
draw them out: to the broads of grass,
say, beside a rat-run island.
Bits of them appear
with the middle days of October:
a bassinette against a wheel,
tarped horses posted up and back,
a pot to simmer the damps
of another year going.

Bargees, they could be,
but with a course
laid secret through the earth.
Windscreens show them
seeming to be about themselves
on the usual levels of the day.
Only someone in the back, maybe,
with a child's distaste for wherefores,
might see them truly,
flowing where they stand,
their past dropped over a tailboard,
the future not even the first twitch
of a dream.

4: The World Was A Squishy And Rubbery Thing...

How Now

I've the look of a man
who doesn't know
if he'll come out where he went in

I sing these days
under my breath
prefer the gaps between words
the moments after things happen

I see
but no memories mass about
thought shows
its usual lump beneath the covers

coming out of a station
say
I may wonder what kind of evening
the sun has struck for us
then drop into it
feel how footsteps trap destinations
how the colours of traffic
splash each other up
from lane to lane

here comes a man hands-free
spraying intimacy onto other breaths
there goes a many-frocked giggle

this woman's had enough of her child
yanks his arm
like a cut of bungee rope
that boy
stands pudgy and baffled
on the eve of his adult life

his face doesn't know
if it should laugh or cry

I could stand forever
in nowheres like this
snapping and deleting

I could die here
furl to a brief aggravation of air
leave my image to sink
like daylight through the waves
an echo
that never used a word

Smile

I'm tired of walking the city,
trying to go nice to nice
with shuttered faces.

I'll stay at home, warm and quiet,
sideways on to the round window
in the closed and twilit porch—

my smile can make what it will
by itself, out and about, a butterfly
over a quay, so to speak, a tickle in the rain.

It might get lucky
with the face of a side-street rambler—
two smiles threading

just for a moment
two freedoms way above the stones,
two snowflakes teasing the dark.

Good luck to my smile
and whatever of joy it may find
whatever of loathing it may have to dodge

like dust
flown clear of a slamming book
on an empty afternoon

good luck to all things that move
though their effort may stir as much
as wind in a time after planets.

When colour depletes
and my porch's window
gives up on show and tell

I'll lift the letterflap
feel my smile
tumbling in under my hand

it will tell me
in its different keys of silence
how it has fared—

hunting through the fissures of the day
making like clown, Samaritan,
peace-patcher—

if it got between a hand and self-removal
sealed a union of the widowed
made someone laugh at a joke like itself,
complete as a ripple,
sudden as a lift of mist

Old Vimto

You stand maybe a dozen yards
from where you parked. The hedges
are full of grey-green waiting. Evening starts.
The dark lifts a corner of the sky.

Wind blows on your face. Not
the old kind that tousled your hair,
invited running freedoms. It fixes
a narrow ache in the middle of your brow.

Circles of beer and wine you remember,
how the optics shone on each round
got in. The glasses have long gone
about the world, stems fogged, handles missing.

The world was a squishy and rubbery thing.
Now it's a stray noise in an empty field.
Nearly empty: you watch a donkey
smuggle its colour into a fence.

All has poured down to this: a hand
pressed for comfort against a pocket of keys,
a frown at the knocking that came and went
behind the dash. An early owl hits its mark

on a high branch and you turn away
to find all your remaindered selves along the hedge
in couples. The lover elaborates
to the high-school boy, who half snorts

and pop-eyes disbelief. The owner of house three
recounts to the callow renter, who plans
avoidance, tries to keep terror
from pursing his lips. At the line's end

the college kid leans down to the round
star-apple face and hands him
a bottle with a straw. Vimto. You can
smell it. Old Vimto. The toast

of the wayfarer squaring fearful up
to his first road. None turns as you walk
slowly past. Your body makes no sound

as you swing in. The wheel shows clean
through your gripping hands. Across the tracker
the miles flow out and vanish into the red.

Shame

The cat calls to me from the garden:
Are you ready for your death?
I've had three lives, could do with
more than nine, if only for how it feels
to wither on the swell, meet myself
coming back. Each time, I flick me to the maggots
as I land in a fresh bed of heartbeats.
I could be leaping the roofs of a runaway train.

                          But you've just the one.
You must walk to that unlit door
with your bag of hurts and history
pulling down a shoulder, as I see them
round here with their Saturday shops
coming back from all their buses—
always with something that leaks,
something meant for the freezer placed aside,
remembered just in time to be thrown out.
Always the wrong sort of something
grabbed in a jostling blur.

                          But for me too
in the end. There'll come a leap, a real cloud-tickler,
that drops me down where the tracks are still singing the train
and the birds of a sudden come over all safe.

Shame, eh?

                The cat vanishes,
a car brakes, someone cries, someone else
claps and whistles. Come evening
he'll be outside the porch,
chewing medicine-grass,
getting his next call ready.

Harbours Hill

One day I shall return to Harbours Hill
and die. On its only street,
cambered, gritted the colour of headache,
against the fall of January stars
I shall let my eyes roll back
to see what my mind makes
of the last quaint shuffle of life...

having looked in the window
of the village's one shop,
how it gathers little marvels
of winter light on stuff it never sells...

having walked the greenish length
of the path beside the unattended church
to see the berries drowse in their blood
between the railing-spikes...

having stood in the church itself
in case the breathing dust
should work loose a word
from a long-immured prayer.

On the only street
at the mouth of the path
I shall set like a tumbler,
my bones brewing a forward roll
so when it comes I fold soundlessly,
ball up where the railings
meet scarps of moss.

Mulch to mulch,
preserved a while
as a randomness of sockets
till the grasses of spring fill my eyes,
lush over the whitened nooks
in which a passenger-spirit
might once have bided its time.

Seven Trees

(Northamptonshire)

I sit in the mist
near the lane's end. All round
are trees I can't name
and never could. My ignorance
is no blight on what they do

or say. Here's one behind me
folding leaves at random
as a little girl visitor,
restless and abashed,
might trouble her hands
at one end of a long sofa.

Caught everywhere in this tree,
let slip in a slightness of wind,
are years of grumbles and sobs
from those who slowed
while passing under
on the run from what was forced
upon their skin
or just as ever hauling their lives
to market.

The branches push the time of day
far back into the sky.
Below them is a kinder weather
in which I'll hide
when the world darkens
and its pulse drops back to mine.

I smile at how once
my mind had to have all and sundry
as claw grips ball
on the legs of tables
that fill high wide forgotten rooms
with bent wood and orphaned smells.

Now my mind is a moment out of nowhere
that forgets when it began
and needs no hour to tell it what it is.
It is this mist, still beyond vacancy,
unhearing the fold of the leaves,
unseeing whatever the lane's end
must turn into.

Stuffage

Stuffage, n. a jokey term for stuff, things; material with which something is stuffed; figuratively, details added to a scene to aid its realism: e.g., in a painting, television series, film.

1.
That's you on the far left
or at least your arm and shoulder
plus a smudge that might be
your head turning
you were toe-to-toe
with immortality
all the others foursquare in shot
went on to rule the world
or anyway hammer its bones
till the birds fled
to the passes of the moon

a shame then
that on the cry of *hold it*
you heard your name
wobbled your place
finding out after
that the name was only almost yours
and anyway belonged
to someone the photograph
hadn't planned to know.

2.
You were fourth anxious customer
tumbling out of the shop
when the coaching-inn next door was surrounded
and the fleshy absconder
lying low as a potman
in the Tudor-village-cum-petting-zoo nearby
was brought to book
you could have stolen all the moment's light
but the chap tumbling out before you

saw fit to pause
and adjust the lie of his trousers

so all the hereafter will chance upon
is a flap of your cagoule
next to a window poster
of rebates and teeth for the aged

series two episode seven it was
with that young American actress
who during a break stepped into the space
where your shy hello was dying
and balanced her laughter on it
at her puppyish co-star
mimicking a tree.

3.
Big do
summer in heels and sweaty humour
Bride's lot or groom's?
demanded a face
made for sputtering pastry
neither
you said and said again—
just trailing a featureless day
through the grounds
so you could watch it being much the same
against a fresh run of houses

the look in his eye seemed to make you
not there
till *Ah* he said *they're on the move*
as organdie and money and tails
massed at a distant lych-gate
Oh he said *there's…damn I should have*
…look could you just hold this?
and he was gone to not listen elsewhere

you still hold this
sometimes it lounges
by the hall telephone
sometimes it scares the shelves

you searched and searched
but he and the rest
had long thrown the dust-sheet
over the church
and all was left again for the likes of you—
coat-backs disappearing
sketches of numbness on upper decks

but this
this will always mesmerise
whether you move it or it moves itself
like a god strayed
from an unknown faith
speaking of those
who have the trick of sunlight
and whistle it to unveil them
wherever they choose to be.

5: Endpapers

i.

it slipped by

the new year
did not come in
it slipped by
on the last street of December

formally dressed
collar and pin
as if summoned to hear
what was no longer
just in the offing
and nod
and see itself out

at all the midnights
stationed through the world
fire-workers crouched at their buttons
champagners gypsied their heels

but the twelve tolls
were the steps of a man
with no head for heights
backing down a long long ladder

time hid beyond
the last reverberation
the new year
pushed that jellied globe aside
straightened a skewed cuff

time shuffled out
fell in step
as they walked
through peach-blossom
summer deeps

the bright cut of days back-endish
Yulelamps chatter-headed in a nave

all bits and dabs
conjured by time
to sweeten the dying way
ended with a gust of old leaves
like a snow-weight absently shaken
absently set down

ii.

Red Ribbons

You make it to an empty bench
outside a pub. The light
keeps turning away
as if the evening sun
is caught among loose change
in a jigging hand. Perhaps
it's the thick-leaved trees
all round the pub garden
chafing day with night
in nearly no wind

many roads from here
wide silences
the hedge-necks of unsigned lanes
yet still you can hear
the last of your parades
disappear down every one
notes from a trumpet
in love with ending and ending—
still make out red ribbons
inflaming the mahogany sky

a young man
joins the next table
is halloo'd and shoulder-clapped
into place. You again
as you were when the ribbons
were cut to their wild mismatches

you put him in a day of yours—
swerving right one time off a crosswalk
and into a barber shop. Got time off?
asked the barber and yes
it was all and only that back then
so little behind you
the weight of nothing in your hands

all about to be about to be
the tall trees casting their branches
obliging the light

iii.

a corner

You turn a corner
and your life bursts into flames
you never used it
now it has up-rushed
the brittle timbers you wedged above

time was you clipped a bit of it
to wear like a gemstone on a pin
thinking that salute enough
to pay it off
for keeping to itself its holy rage

you walked in seemliness
it wept in dripping places
enough
now it climbs you like lizards
melts heart and breath

as with the fires
of all the stars you missed
the evenings they tenanted
long over now
long toppled into the nowhere seas

on this street you stand and burn
no-one can help you
distracted as they are
by keeping one scorch ahead
of their own end

mothers pull their children to their breasts
and scramble
as from a drunk
stripped off to challenge the sun
with his matchstick of light

iv.

the hedges at the end of the lane

the hedges
at the end of the lane
the swallows in the sky
little friends
pedalling fast into the park

were.
But what now, what
do we do?
turn off the radio
to save the batteries

wait for
the next announcement
in an hour as they say
squash ourselves to stuff
in the angles

of walls remaining
find we daren't close our eyes
daren't keep them open
fight the evil tease
of memory   of breath

there will be no announcement
there is no hour
only dead bikes in the trees
tatterings of wing on umber waters

the next we hear
will be the raging stumble
of a looter
too late for his greed
coming sudden
on his unhallowed pit

v.

the slowing of your blood

You meet a donkey on the road.
The donkey stops. There is snow
in the air so you both should get on
but you do not. You look
into the donkey's eyes and he looks
into yours. You reach
to stroke his nose. He twitches
flicks his ears but a moment later
his head is down and his nose
is pressed to your stomach.
So you both stand. The snow comes on.
You see the flakes between his ears
perhaps he feels the slowing of your blood.

Didn't someone say once that
on the way from morning to his bespoke end
he found himself of a sudden
in the middle of a deep dark wood?
He probably took bearings of a kind
had a word with himself and pushed on.
You and the donkey do not.
Perhaps you or he are a freckle's width
from knowing why
but you leave that where it is
if it is. The snow keeps on
the donkey lifts his head
you stretch either hand to still it.
You look into his eyes and he
looks into yours.
And now there is no road.

6: Motley Futures...

Look At The Child

If the church had a lawn
seeded on a slope
he could exercise the buggy
and the child that isn't there,
also walk them crossways
between the vicar's wall
with its overhang of mist
and the far side of the grounds
where the relicts bloom.

As it is he can only show the child
to other perimeter people,
women with blown-rose faces
stood with care between a shelter
and its hill of glass,
a loafer turning back from a gulley
the council has whimsically sealed
or slipping late from a valley of retail
as electric gates roll home.

The tilt of the buggy says look,
look there,
wouldn't he be beautiful?
wouldn't his face be the only book
you need open? See how all he will know
dusts over his eyes already,
how his mouth laughs and cries
in its stillness. Listen to all the years
of his breath.

Sometimes the girls bend down
and reach with baffled fingers,
straighten up into their mothers
for as long as a bird divides the sun—

knowing what they do not know,
planning to giggle
but finding instead as they turn away
a nameless colour in their world,
a different press of breeze upon their skin.

Preserves

The night is given up to owls
in rowan trees across the plains of England.
Here and there, through long-ungirded counties,
green lanes find fellowships of light:
a hostel-church, maybe, a stately home
grown up at last, at last set usefully
to warm and feed
a hundred of the earth's inheritors.

Here and there stand the freak-shrines,
chirruping with odd-me-dods
from floor to beam:
a square face of blue pulses
that eats and spews eternally a single plastic card,
shrieks *Do You Need More Time?* as a clown might,
sat in sawdust. An iron-work tree
leaved with excavated mobiles
kept in juice enough to wink their long-gones
like tiny portraits under attic webs:
Me in Frisco lol. Chamonix—gr8.
Arrabiatafest wiv Greg.
Greg's bruv [phwoary-sweaty-tongue face].
Separate from the rest,
some grandfather iPad sobs *no network*
on a bed of charnel plush.

The night is given up
to children who crowd the shrines,
whose wisdom works already
on a different, proper future.
Still they wonder
at a time when the world yelled so long
for its mammy,
louder, more fearful than they could ever be,
and would not shush.

Feste Packs

(Twelfth Night)

1

'A sister,' says Olivia, 'you are she.'
Viola giggles, takes Orsino's hand
while Sebastian lurks, grins, looks . . . well, married.
And so the whirligig of toffs brings in
its closure. Time I wasn't here, although
I've been requested (in the way that kind
request) to derry-down at their big feast.
Well . . . no . . . besides, some of the others have
cleared out already. An hour since, Fabian
took horse, a deep pouch at his waist clanking
as cloth does not, as pewter dishes do.
Sir Andrew's long gone: maundering the way
to his estate with empty heart and purse.
Toby, of course, will stay for whatever
he can push at that gross mouth—capon, sack,
wench's quim—till Maria spots his game
and shrieks, explodes, flails, gets them both slung out.

2

Did no one hear the sulphur words he flung
back at our faces as those yellow legs
spindled him off? Does no-one have a care
for ends untied, for prayer without amen?
He'll come after me first—and last, maybe,
making me serve the pack's turn. Even now,
I'd guess, he's down the city's rabbit-holes,
a fist of tankard-pay for each soldier
inert between our wars and keen enough
to keep in trim with midnight clutch-and-slice.
Can't blame him—well I can, I hate him—still,
the joke was winded from the start, and yet
I dived straight in, tormented, gurned—ah yes,
occasion was ministered and I fell
exactly as the doormat steward sneered
that time before my lady. Damn his truth,
damn jokery. Damn all this.

3

                                        Packing up?
A moment's work when you have nothing more
than one change of jerkin and hose to roll
beneath your arm, odd bits of maying rhyme
and flash quibble to tuck inside your head.
I might, while daylight holds, take one last tour
of Olivia's lush parts: the spinney
where I'd sleep under last night's tavern-load,
the park where I'd sing death to come away
and death would snort and cry, not likely, boy,
you've years tied to your tin-pot minstrelsy
before my appetites alight on you.
Forget that. The terrace, then, I'll stand there
a few vague moments. Nothing I love more
than colonnades with sunlight failing west.

4

And after that? Sir Andrew. Yes, I'll track
the long throw of his lanky shadow, sit
beside him halfway up his hundred steps.
Unbow his head, or try, with my best songs
for patching hearts split double-fold by love
untendered, friendship made a pool of piss—
Belch's sour malice when the jig was up,
the sailing disregard of my lady
as was. Go, I'll advise, seek out the shores
of seas tropic and icebound, passes through
mountains whose air outdoes a drum of sack.
Stand still and stare, think nothing save for how
you were (you told us) adored once. Perhaps
you'll happen on that lady at some strand
or by a lantern'd bridge when day's played out.
Fantastical? How so? Consider all
the fairy doings we were caught in. Still,
if not, no matter. Bear on with a care
for your mending spirit. Be civil but
be strange. Friendship does not rattle its glass
and furl the bill's dry numbers in your own.
Your smile, salute—these are portable. Give,
yes, but giving done, take both back. Goodnight
should always play the shepherd to goodbye.

5

And then for me a journey too, a song
to baffle time and space. I'll swing off through
the changeful ages, scramble up and down
the future's hills. Seek out all those who are
as I was, mud-holed at a story's end,
unable to break *finis* down and step
into their true pace, own their tomorrows.
Feel, I'll whisper, how the wind disarrays
your coat, how the rain muslins your sad eyes
enchantingly. No tall yarn prisons them.
Even as we talk they play plait-the-grass
and splash-the-skull round certain faceless tombs
of some to whom I bowed and some with whom
I shat life like crow-pellets. Take my hand . . .
up . . . easy . . . up. We'll walk to the next rise
and you will see the plains and valleys of
time after tales. I'd say you'll find, like me,
that dust-broad highways mix contrariwise
with sloughs. But all is yours to age along.
Just train the corner of your eye to note
the tree that bends upon a ridge, the cloud
preparing ebony confusion on
the downlands. What breathes in and over them
tousled Eden and will only go out
with the sun. Here we are. Look on your miles,
take your step. I'm this way. Mind how you live.

Come With Me

Come with me
for the morning has tumbled into its colours
the day waits like your reflection in the sink
tremoring with *yes*.

Come with me on a train ride
from who knows where
to who knows when
pulling in at upland stations
as noon breaks over the hills.

Or we might happen on a tribe
at the twist of a path in a forest
landed that moment from another age
who know as much about us
as a flagstone knows of a church
but still shake hands and offer wine.

Come with me and watch time's clock
flip back to zero at fall of dusk
clearing the way for tomorrow
with fresh magic on the wind
the world at your door starting over.

Acknowledgements

The author would like to thank the editors of the following magazines, in which a number of these poems have appeared:

Brittle Star
Coachlines
Crossroads (Poland)
Dream-Catcher
The Interpreter's House
London Grip
Magazine Six (Key West, USA)
Pennine Platform
Poetry on Loan
Under the Radar
Whispering Dialogue

'Bikes' won first prize, Cheltenham Poetry Buzzwords Competition, 2015. 'Shrawley Cross' appears in The Poetry of Worcestershire *(Offa's Press, 2019).*

About The Author

"Since 2004, Dr. Michael Wyndham Thomas has helped develop and spearhead the workshops for the Key West Robert Frost Poetry Festival. His hands-on teaching skills make poetry exciting for even the novice; his depth of knowledge is impressive.

"Because he has endeared himself to everyone associated with the festival—and to many others who live on this island at the southernmost point in the United States—Michael is fondly referred to as the Poet at Large in the Conch Republic Navy"—Barbara Bowers, writer and journalist.

Many thanks from The Robert Frost Poetry Festival Committee, Key West, Florida.

Novels
The Mercury Annual (TQF / Theaker's Paperback Library, 2009)
Pilgrims at the White Horizon (TQF / Theaker's Paperback Library, 2013)

Short fiction
The Portswick Imp: Collected Stories, 2001-2016 (Black Pear Press, 2018)

Poetry collections
God's Machynlleth and Other Poems (Flarestack, 1996)
Port Winston Mulberry (Littlejohn and Bray, 2009)
Batman's Hill, South Staffs (Flipped Eye International, 2013)
The Girl from Midfoxfields (Black Pear Press, 2014)
Come To Pass (Oversteps Books, 2014)
Early and Late (Cairn Time Press, 2018)
Featured in Polly Stretton, ed, *The Unremembered: World War One's Army of Workers, The British Story* (Black Pear Press, 2018)

Drama

Assumption Eve (Worcester Commandery, 2000)
FAQ (The Progress Theatre Festival, Reading, 2009, and the Shoebox Theatre Company, Staffordshire, 2011)
When? (The Blue Orange Theatre, Birmingham [Shoebox Theatre Company], 2011)

Novella

Esp. Shortlisted for the UK Novella Award (2015)

Essays and Reviews

Critical Survey, Crossroads, English, The English Review,
The Explicator, Irish Studies Review, The Irish University Review,
The Journal of American Haiku, The London Magazine, No Limits,
Other Poetry, Staple Magazine, The Times Literary Supplement,
Under the Radar (1996-present)

www.michaelwthomas.co.uk

The Swan Village Reporter:

http://swansreport.blogspot.co.uk